First Facts®

Spiders

Wolf Spiders

by Joanne Mattern

Consultant:
Pedro Barbosa, PhD
Department of Entomology
University of Maryland, College Park

CAPSTONE PRESS
a capstone imprint

First Facts is published by Capstone Press,
151 Good Counsel Drive, P.O. Box 669, Mankato, Minnesota 56002.
www.capstonepub.com

Books published by Capstone Press are manufactured with paper
containing at least 10 percent post-consumer waste.

Library of Congress Cataloging-in-Publication Data
Mattern, Joanne, 1963–
  Wolf spiders / by Joanne Mattern.
      p. cm.—(First facts. Spiders)
  Includes bibliographical references and index.
  Summary: "A brief introduction to wolf spiders, including their habitat, food, and
life cycle"—Provided by publisher.
  ISBN 978-1-4296-4523-2 (library binding)
  1. Wolf spiders—Juvenile literature. I. Title. II. Series.
  QL458.42.L9M33 2011
  595.4'4—dc22
                          2010002259

Editorial Credits
Lori Shores, editor; Veronica Correia, designer; Eric Manske, production specialist

Photo Credits
Alamy/Arco Images GmbH, 5
Dreamstime/kenneystudios/Teresa Kenney, 7; Lnzyx (Yongxin Zhang), 1
James P. Rowan, 8
Pete Carmichael, 6, 11, 13, 15, 19, 21
Shutterstock/Cathy Keifer, cover; Jerome Whittingham, 20; orionmystery@flickr, 16

Essential content terms are **bold** and are defined at the bottom of the page
where they first appear.

Table of Contents

Speedy Hunters

Wolf spiders get their name because they are active hunters. Like wolves, wolf spiders chase their **prey**. They run fast to catch insects and other spiders.

Spider Fact!

Wolves hunt in groups called packs. But wolf spiders hunt alone.

prey—an animal hunted by another animal for food

5

Hairy Bodies

Most wolf spiders are less than 1 inch (2.5 centimeters) long. The Carolina wolf spider is the largest wolf spider in North America. This spider measures more than 3 inches (7.6 cm) long.

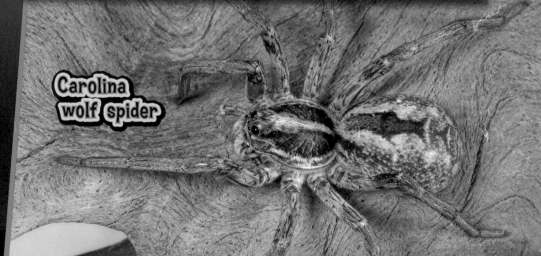

Carolina wolf spider

cephalothorax

abdomen

Wolf spiders are **arachnids**. They have two main body parts and eight legs. Their bodies are covered with black, brown, or gray hair. Some wolf spiders have stripes on their backs and legs.

arachnid—an animal with four pairs of legs and no backbone, wings, or antennae

Looking Good

Eight eyes help wolf spiders see better than most other spiders. Their large front eyes help them see in the dark. Four small eyes look out from below their large eyes. Two small eyes look up from the top of their heads.

Spider Fact!

A wolf spider can look four different ways at once.

Spider World

More than 2,000 kinds of wolf spiders live all over the world. In the United States, there are more than 100 kinds of wolf spiders.

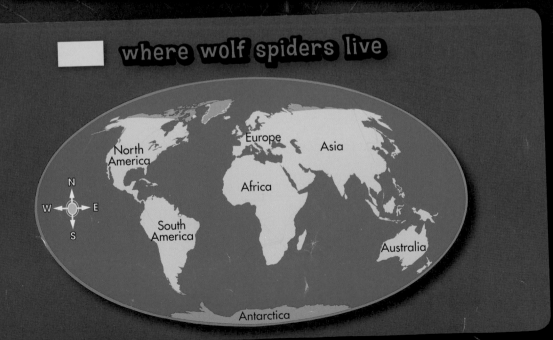

where wolf spiders live

Wolf spiders live in woods, fields, and swamps. Some wolf spiders live in deserts. Others live on mountains. Wolf spiders even live near the Arctic Ocean.

Spider Homes

Wolf spiders usually live in underground **burrows**. They line the inside of their burrows with **silk**. Wolf spiders use twigs and leaves to hide their burrows from enemies.

Spider Fact!

Wolf spiders sometimes take over insects' burrows.

burrow—a tunnel or hole in the ground where an animal lives
silk—a string made by spiders

burrow

Hunting and Eating

Wolf spiders hunt during the day and at night. A hungry wolf spider sneaks up on an insect. The spider quickly jumps and bites the insect with sharp **fangs**. **Venom** flows through the fangs to kill the prey.

Spider Fact!

Wolf spiders eat ants, flies, beetles, and grasshoppers. They even eat other spiders.

fang—a long, pointed toothlike mouthpart
venom—a harmful liquid produced by some animals

15

egg sac

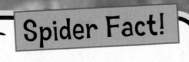

Spider Fact!

Female wolf spiders
protect their eggs from
hungry insects.

Mother Spiders

In the summer, male and female wolf spiders join together to produce young. Then the female lays about 100 eggs. She wraps the eggs in an **egg sac**. The sac sticks to her body. The mother spider carries the sac everywhere she goes.

After a few weeks, the female bites a hole in the egg sac. The **spiderlings** crawl out and climb onto their mother's back. The mother carries them for one week. After that, the spiderlings take care of themselves.

Spider Fact!

Spiderlings hold on to hairs on their mother's body.

spiderling—a young spider

Life Cycle of a Wolf Spider

Newborn

Spiderlings can bite as soon as they are born.

spiderlings

Young

Wolf spiders shed their outer skeletons many times as they grow.

Adult

Wolf spiders can live for up to five years.

Staying Safe

Birds, snakes, and frogs eat wolf spiders. The spiders usually run away, but they also hide. Their colors help them hide against the ground, a leaf, or a tree.

Wolf spiders use vibrations to find prey. Their body hairs sense the smallest movements around them. A wolf spider can feel an insect's wings beating. It can even sense an ant walking by.

Glossary

arachnid (uh-RACK-nid)—an animal with four pairs of legs and no backbone, wings, or antennae

burrow (BUHR-oh)—a tunnel or hole in the ground where an animal lives

egg sac (EG SAK)—a small pouch made of silk that holds spider eggs

fang (FANG)—a long, pointed toothlike mouthpart

prey (PRAY)—an animal hunted by another animal for food

silk (SILK)—a string made by spiders

spiderling (SPYE-dur-ling)—a young spider

venom (VEN-uhm)—a harmful liquid produced by some animals

vibration (vye-BRAY-shuhn)—a fast movement back and forth; vibrations in the ground and air are made when people or animals move

Read More

Bishop, Nic. *Spiders.* New York: Scholastic Nonfiction, 2007.

Hartley, Karen, Chris Macro, and Philip Taylor. *Spider.* Bug Books. Chicago: Heinemann Library, 2008.

Goldish, Meish. *Spooky Wolf Spiders.* No Backbone! New York: Bearport Publishing, 2009.

Internet Sites

FactHound offers a safe, fun way to find Internet sites related to this book. All of the sites on FactHound have been researched by our staff.

Here's all you do:

Visit *www.facthound.com*

FactHound will fetch the best sites for you!

Index